Also by Heinrich Böll

18 Stories

Irish Journal

End of a Mission

The Clown

Billiards at Half-Past Nine

Group Portrait with Lady

Absent Without Leave

Adam *and* The Train (And Where Were You,
Adam? *and* The Train Was on Time)

The Lost Honor of Katharina Blum

The Bread of Those Early Years

Children Are Civilians Too

Missing Persons and Other Essays

And Never Said a Word

The Safety Net

What's to Become
of the Boy?

What's to Become of the Boy?

—— or ——

Something to Do with Books

HEINRICH BÖLL

Translated by Leila Vennewitz

ALFRED A. KNOPF   NEW YORK   1984

My warm thanks to my husband, William, whose skill, knowledge, and patience have contributed so much to this translation.

Leila Vennewitz

THIS IS A BORZOI BOOK PUBLISHED BY
ALFRED A. KNOPF, INC.

Copyright © 1984 by Heinrich Böll
and Leila Vennewitz

LIBRARY OF CONGRESS CATALOGING
IN PUBLICATION DATA
Böll, Heinrich. [*date*]
What's to become of the boy?
Translation of:
Was soll aus dem Jungen bloss werden?
1. Böll, Heinrich, [*date*]—Biography—Youth.
2. Authors, German—20th century—Biography.
I. Title.
PT2603.O394Z47613   1984   833'.914 [B]   83–49087
ISBN 0–394–53016–0

Manufactured in the United States of America
First American Edition

Frontispiece: Heinrich Böll during his school years.

For Samay, Sara,
and Boris

What's to Become of the Boy?

1

ON JANUARY 30, 1933, I was fifteen years and six weeks old, and almost exactly four years later, on February 6, 1937, when I was nineteen years and seven weeks old, I graduated from high school with a "Certificate of Maturity." This certificate contains two errors: my date of birth is incorrect, and my choice of career—"book trade"—was altered by the school principal, without consulting me, to "publishing," I have no idea why. These two errors, which I cherish, justify me in regarding all the other particulars, including my grades, with some skepticism.

I didn't discover either of these errors until two years later, when, as the 1939 university summer term was about to begin, I looked at the certificate before handing it in to the University of Cologne and discovered the incorrect birth date. It would never have occurred to me to have an error of that kind in such a solemn official document corrected: that error permits me to entertain a certain doubt as to whether I am really the person who is certified thereon as mature. Might the document refer to someone else? If so, to whom? This little game also allows me to consider the possibility that the entire document may be invalid.

There are a few further points that I must clarify.
If it should be regarded as mandatory for German
authors to have "suffered" under the school system, I
must once again appear to have failed in my duty. Of
course I suffered (do I hear a voice: "Who, old or
young, does not suffer"?), but not in school. I main-
tain that I never let things get that far. I dealt with
each problem as it arose, as I so often did in later life,
aware of the implications. How, is something I shall
explain later. I did find the transition from elementary
to high school briefly painful, but I was ten at the time,
so this is not relevant to the period I wish to describe.
I was sometimes bored in school, annoyed, chiefly by
our religion teacher (and he, of course by me: such
comments are to be interpreted bilaterally), but did I
"suffer"? No. Further clarification: my unconquerable
(and still unconquered) aversion to the Nazis was not
revolt: *they* revolted *me*, repelled me on every level of
my existence: conscious *and* instinctive, aesthetic *and*
political. To this day I have been unable to find any
entertaining, let alone aesthetic, dimension to the Nazis
and their era, a fact that makes me shudder when I
see certain film and stage productions. I simply *could
not* join the Hitler Youth, I did not join it, and that
was that.

A further clarification (there is yet another to
come!): justifiable mistrust of my memory. All this
happened forty-eight to forty-four years ago, and I

have no notes or jottings to resort to; they were burned or blown to bits in an attic of 17 Karolinger-Ring in Cologne. Moreover, I am no longer sure of how some of my personal experiences synchronize with historical events. For example, I would have bet almost anything that it was in the fall of 1934 that Göring, in his capacity as Prime Minister of Prussia, caused seven young Communists of Cologne to be beheaded with an ax. I would have lost that bet: it was the fall of 1933. And my memory doesn't betray me when I recall that one morning a schoolmate of mine, a member of the black-uniformed S.S., exhausted yet with the hectic light of the chase still in his eyes, told me they had spent the night scouring the villas of Godesberg for the former cabinet minister Treviranus. Thank God (as I, not he, thought) without success. But when, to make quite sure, I proceed to look it up, I find that Treviranus had already emigrated by 1933; in 1933, the minimum age for membership in the S.S. was eighteen, though we were only sixteen then; thus, this memory cannot be placed earlier than 1935 or 1936. In other words, either Treviranus must have reentered the German Reich illegally in 1935 or 1936, or the S.S. must have been fed wrong information. The story itself—that strange blend of exhaustion and eyes shining with the light of the chase—I can vouch for, but I cannot place it.

Final clarification or, if you prefer, warning: the title *What's to Become of the Boy?* should arouse

neither false hopes nor false fears. Not every boy
whose family and friends have reason to ask them-
selves and him this eternally apprehensive question
does, after various delays and roundabout approaches,
eventually become a writer; and I would like to stress
that, at the time it was put, this question was both
serious and warranted. In fact, I am not sure whether
my mother, were she still alive, wouldn't still be asking
the same question today: "What's to become of the
boy?" Perhaps there are times when we should be
asking it about elderly and successful politicians,
church dignitaries, writers, et cetera.

2

So it is somewhat warily that I now enter upon
the "realistic," the chronologically confused path,
wary of my own and other people's autobiographical
pronouncements. The mood and the situation I can
vouch for, also the facts bound up with moods and
situations; but, confronted with verifiable historical
facts, I cannot vouch for the synchronization, as wit-
ness the above examples.

I simply don't remember whether in January 1933
I was still or no longer a member of a Marian youth
fellowship; nor would it be accurate if I were to say

that I had "gone to school" for four years under Nazi rule. For I did *not* go to school for four years; there were, if not countless, certainly uncounted days when —apart from vacations, holidays, sickness, which must in any case be deducted—I didn't go to school at all. I loved what I might call the "school of the streets" (I can't say "school of the bushes," since Cologne's old town has little, and never had much, in the way of bushes). Those streets between the Waidmarkt and the cathedral, the side streets off the Neumarkt and the Heumarkt, all the streets going right and left down to the cathedral from Hohe Strasse: how I loved roaming around in the town, sometimes not even taking my schoolbag along as an alibi but leaving it at home among the galoshes and long overcoats in the hall closet. Long before I knew Anouilh's play *Traveller without Luggage*, that was what I enjoyed being, and I still dream of being one. Hands in pockets, eyes open, street hawkers, pedlars, markets, churches, museums (yes, I loved the museums, I was hungry for education, even if not very assiduous in its pursuit), prostitutes (in Cologne there was hardly a street without them) —dogs and cats, nuns and priests, monks—and the Rhine, that great gray river, alive and lively, beside which I could sit for hours at a time; I used to sit in movie theaters too, in the dusk of the early performances that were frequented by a few idlers and unemployed people. My mother knew a lot, suspected

some things but not all. According to family rumors—
which, like all family rumors, must be taken with a
grain of salt—during the last three years of those four
Nazi school years, I spent less than half the time in
school. Yes, those were my school days, but I didn't
spend all my days in school, so that in trying to describe those four years, I can only make an "also"
tale out of them, for the fact is that I "also" went to
school.

3

FORTY-EIGHT YEARS going back, from 1981 to
1933, and four years going forward, from 1933 to
1937: in this leapfrog procession some things must fall
by the wayside. The man of sixty-three smiles down
upon the boy of fifteen, but the boy of fifteen does not
smile up at the man of sixty-three, and it is here, in
this unilateral perspective which is not matched by a
corresponding perspective on the part of the fifteen-
year-old, that we must expect to find a source of error.

On January 30, 1933, the fifteen-year-old is ill in
bed with a severe case of flu, victim of an epidemic
that I consider to have been given insufficient consideration in analyses of Hitler's seizure of power. It is a
fact that public life was partially paralyzed, many
schools and government offices were closed, at least

locally and regionally. One of my classmates brought me the news as I lay sick in bed. In those days we still had no radio, and homemade efforts to build crystal sets hadn't yet begun. We didn't acquire the mini-edition of the so-called people's radio until shortly before the outbreak of war, our reluctance almost out-weighing the necessity. After a second move within two years, we were now living at 32 Maternus-Strasse, facing the dismal rear wall of what was then the engineering school. Nevertheless, we were not very far from the Rhine, and from our corner bay window we could see the neo-Gothic, tri-gabled warehouse of the Rhenus Line, of which I painted innumerable water colors. Just around the corner was Römer Park, a little farther on, Hindenburg Park, where on fine days my mother could sit among the jobless or people who had been forced into early retirement.

I lay in bed and read—probably Jack London, whose works we borrowed in the book club edition from a friend, but it is also possible—oh raised eyebrows of the literary connoisseurs, how gladly I would smooth you down!—that I was *simultaneously* reading Trakl. The great tiled stove in our corner room had, for once, been lit, and from it, using a long paper spill, I took a light for my (forbidden) cigarette. My mother's comment on the appointment of Hitler: "That's war," or maybe it was: "Hitler, that means war."

The news of Hitler's appointment came as no surprise. After Hindenburg's "shameful betrayal" of
Brüning (that's what my father called it), after von
Papen and Schleicher, Hindenburg was obviously
capable of anything. That strange (to this day still
somewhat obscure) affair known at the time as the
"Eastern agricultural support scandal," on which even
our extremely reticent *Kölnische Volkszeitung* had
reported, had deprived "the venerable old field mar-
shal" of the last shred of what had been at best mini-
mal credit—not politically, merely the shred of moral
credit that people had been willing to attribute to his
"Prussian integrity."

My mother hated Hitler from the very beginning
(unfortunately she didn't live to see his death); she
dubbed him *Rövekopp*, "turnip head," an allusion to
the traditional St. Martin's torches roughly carved
from sugar beets and leaving, wherever possible, something resembling a moustache. Hitler—he was beyond
discussion, and his long-time delegate in Cologne, a
certain Dr. Robert Ley (try to imagine a character like
Ley later in control of the entire German work force!),
had done little to render Hitler and his Nazis worthy
of discussion: they were nothing more than the "howl-
ing void," without the human dimension that might
have merited the term "rabble." The Nazis were "not
even rabble." My mother's war theory was hotly
denied: the fellow wouldn't even last long enough to

be able to start a war. (As the world discovered to its
consternation, he lasted long enough.)

I forget how long I had to stay in bed. The flu
epidemic gave a modest boost to the liquor stores;
cheap rum was in demand—in the form of grog, it was
said to offer cure or prevention. We bought moderate
quantities of it in a shop at the corner of Bonner-
Strasse and Darmstädter-Strasse: the proprietor's
name was, I believe, Volk, and he had a son with
flaming red hair who went to our school. I forget
whether the burning of the Reichstag building, the
"excellent timing" of which was noted by many, occurred while I was still sick or during term time or
even during vacation (at some point there must have
also been the Carnival!). In any event, before the
March election I was going back to school; and only
after that election—one so easily forgets that the re-
sults just barely provided a majority for a coalition
between Nazis and the German National Party—in
April or May the first Hitler Youth shirts appeared in
school, and one or two Storm Trooper uniforms in the
higher grades.

There was also—I forget exactly when—a book-
burning, an embarrassing, in fact a pathetic, exercise.
The Nazi flag was hoisted, but I can't remember anyone making a speech, hurling anathemas at title after
title, author after author, tossing books into the fire.
The books must have been placed there, a little heap,

in advance, and since that book-burning I know that
books don't burn well. Someone must have forgotten
to pour gasoline over them. I also find it hard to
imagine that the modest library of our high school
(which, although called the Kaiser Wilhelm State
High School, was extremely Catholic) could have contained much "decadent" literature. The background of
virtually the whole student body was lower middle
class with few "excrescences" either upward or down-
ward. It's possible that one or other of the teachers
privately sacrificed his Remarque or his Tucholsky to
feed the funeral pyre. Be that as it may, none of these
authors was listed in the curriculum; and after the
tangible, the visible and audible, barbarities occurring
between January 30 and the Reichstag fire—increasingly so between Reichstag fire and March election—
this act of *symbolic* barbarity was perhaps not all that
impressive.

The nonsymbolic purges were visible and audible,
were tangible: Social Democrats disappeared (Soll-
mann, Görlinger, and others), as did politicians of
the Catholic Center Party and, needless to say, Communists, and it was no secret that the Storm Troopers
were establishing concentration camps in the fortifications around Cologne's Militär-Ring: expressions such
as "protective custody" and "shot while trying to
escape" became familiar; even some of my father's
friends were caught up in the process, men who later,

on their return, maintained a stony silence. Paralysis spread, an atmosphere of fear prevailed, and the Nazi hordes, brutal and bloodthirsty, saw to it that the terror was not confined to rumors.

The streets left and right off Severin-Strasse, along which I walked to school (Alteburger-Strasse, Silvan-Strasse, Severin-Strasse, Perlen-Graben), constituted a far from "politically reliable" area. There were days, after the Reichstag fire and before the March election, when the area was entirely or partially cordoned off, the least reliable streets being those to the right of Severin-Strasse. Who was that woman screaming on Achter-Gässchen, who that man screaming on Landsberg-Strasse, who on Rosen-Strasse? Perhaps it is not in school but on our way to school that we learn lessons for life. It was obvious that along those streets, people were being beaten up, dragged out of their front doors. After the Reichstag fire and the March election it grew quieter, but it was still far from quiet. One must not forget that, after the November 1932 election, the Communist Party had become the second-strongest party in a city as Catholic as Cologne (Center Party 27.3 percent; Communists 24.5 percent; Nazis 20.5 percent; Social Democrats 17.5 percent), a state of affairs somewhat similar to that in Italy

today. Despite its Catholic reputation and all the cleri-
cal machinations, Cologne was and still is a progres-
sive city. Then in March 1933 the Nazis obtained 33.3
percent, the Center Party still as much as 25.6 percent,
and the Communists and Social Democrats, despite terror and purges, 18.1 and 14.9 percent: the "unreliable
area" was still far from being "normalized," there was
plenty of work left for the Storm Troopers to do.
(There would be a lot more to say about Cologne, but
in my opinion, after the Cathedral Jubilee, Pope John
Paul II's visit, and the Ludwig Museum, Cologne has
had ample publicity. Moreover, the Rhine flows on.)

It must have been about this time that the father
of one of my older sister's school friends, a quiet,
reliable police officer with a Center Party background,
took early retirement because he could no longer stand
the sight of the "bloody towels" in his precinct: those,
too, were not symbolic signs; the "bloody towels" were
related to the screams I had heard from Achter-
Gässchen, from Rosen-Strasse and Landsberg-Strasse.

By now it will have become increasingly evident
to the reader that, as far as school is concerned, this is
no more than an "also" story, that, although it deals
with my school days, it doesn't deal only with the days
I spent in school. Although school was far from being
a minor issue, it was not a primary issue during those
four years.

.   .   .

A clean-up operation of a quite different kind brought considerable changes in my daily walk to school: the crackdown on the cigarette smugglers who stood at street corners or in doorways whispering offers of "Dutch merchandise." The cheapest legally acquired cigarette cost at least two and a half pfennigs, a feeble object, half as firmly packed as a Juno or an Eckstein, which cost three and a third pfennigs each. The Dutch product was pale gold, firm, a third plumper than an Eckstein, and was offered at one to one and a half pfennigs each. Naturally that was very enticing at a time when Brüning's penny-pinching policies were still having their effect, so my brother Alois would sometimes give me money to buy him illegal Dutch cigarettes. Between Rosen-Strasse and Perlen-Graben, the focal point being somewhere around Landsberg-Strasse, with scattered outposts extending as far as the Eulen-Garten (the smugglers' headquarters that were located close to our school on Heinrich-Strasse), I had to be both wary and alert, had to appear both confidence-inspiring and eager to buy. Apparently I succeeded, and that early training or schooling (which, as I say, cannot be acquired in school but only on the way to school), that education, if you prefer, turned out to be very useful to me in later years in many of the black markets of Europe. (I have dealt elsewhere with the fact that a dedicated feeling for legality does not form part of the Cologne attitude to life.)

So the Dutch merchandise would reach home safe
and sound, and I would receive my cut in the form of
fragrant cigarettes. On one occasion, I must admit, I
was diddled: the neat little package with its Dutch
revenue stamp contained, instead of twenty-five cigarettes, approximately twenty-five grams of . . . potato
peelings! To this day I fail to understand *why* potato
peelings, and not, say, sawdust or woodshavings. They
had been carefully weighed, evenly distributed, packed
in foil. (Contempt for wax seals, lead seals, bailiff's
seals, revenue stamps—also a kind of seal—ingrained
in me by my mother, turned out, after the war, to be
my undoing when I broke the seal of an electricity
meter and tampered with it—unfortunately in a de-
tectable manner. Bailiff's seals were promptly removed
as a matter of course.) I was enjoined by my brother
in future to check the goods and was still puzzling
over *how,* since everything had to be done so quickly,
when suddenly the entire smuggling operation was
smashed. Certain streets were virtually under siege,
and I recall at least one armored vehicle. Police and
customs agents—in the end without shooting—cleared
out the whole smugglers' nest: there were rumors of
millions of confiscated cigarettes and numerous arrests.

4

Y ES, *school*, I know—I'll get back to that. I was still
in the eighth grade, and my route to school became
even quieter. For a time I must have been walking with
my head down, since one day my father offered me a
prize if I could name twenty-five stores between St.
Severin's Church and Perlen-Graben. I lifted my head
once again and won the prize: I also lifted my head to
read *Der Stürmer,* the newspaper in its display case
outside the former trade-union building on Severin-
Strasse, not far from the corner that goes off to Perlen-
Graben. What I read did not enhance my sympathies
for the Nazis. (Today, alas, that area is a desert; war
and the Nord-Süd freeway saw to that. Yet that little
square outside the Church of St. John the Baptist used
to be bustling with life.)

Not always with the prior but always with the sub-
sequent approval of my mother, I went often to the
school of the streets. (As reported elsewhere, my
mother anyway used to run a kind of center for non-
family truants under the coffee grinder that hung on
the kitchen wall.) So, if I went to the school of the
streets, it wasn't because my high school was particularly Nazist or Nazi-tainted. It was not, and I remember most of my teachers without any resentment

at all. I don't even feel resentment toward our teacher
of religion, although I argued with him—to the point of
being kicked out of the classroom. The points of dis-
pute were not the Nazis; on that score he was not
vulnerable. On the contrary, I recall an excellent lec-
ture he gave on the sentimental and commercial background to the Day of the German Mother. What
aroused my ire was the overriding bourgeois element
in his teaching. It was against this that I rebelled so
inarticulately; he had no idea what I meant or how I
meant it, he was more confused than angry.

The cause of my rebellion could be found in the totally
indefinable social situation in which we found ourselves: had our financial plight lowered our social
status or made us classless? To this day I don't know.
We were neither true lower middle class nor conscious
proletarians, and we had a strong streak of the Bohemian. "Bourgeois" had become a dirty word for us. The
elements of those three classes, to none of which we
truly belonged, had made what might be called "bourgeois" Christianity absolutely insufferable to us. Our
teacher of religion probably never understood what I
had in mind, and I probably didn't express it clearly
enough. (Obviously the author has always irked, and
been irked by, church and state. And, being a true son
of Cologne, he has never taken secular and ecclesiasti-

cal authority very seriously, much less regarded them as important!)

Merely lowered socially or truly classless? The question remains unanswered. The other subjects, aside from religion? I can't remember anything special about them. Even in those days I was gradually starting to "orchestrate" school. And, since I did respect the intelligence of our teacher of religion, who, although bourgeois to the marrow, made no concessions to the Nazis, I began from time to time to attend school mass in the Franciscan Church on Ulrich-Gasse. It made for a change in my usual route along Rosen-Strasse. As for the church, I found it (no other word occurs to me) disgusting, with its corny statues and decorations and the stale smells emanating from the congregation. There is only one word for those smells: *fug*, trying to pass itself off as fervor. I went there quite pointedly, with only occasionally the aim of offering some slight consolation to our teacher of religion, since I certainly didn't hate him: it was just that sometimes we had violent arguments. He obviously suffered from high blood pressure, and some of the boys in the Hitler Youth couldn't resist taking advantage of him: not on their own—they could have done that before 1933—but by virtue of their uniforms and potential rank (there was all that braid!). He was helpless and unsuspecting, had no idea that their attitude was a mark of the "bourgeois" element's turning against

him, that the boys who, until March 1933, had been
good young Catholics now were sniffing the "new age"
and intended to make the most of it. This harassment
didn't last long, nor did it get worse; it soon died
down, but our last lessons with him, barely three years
later, were terrible, though for quite different reasons.
No doubt he still considered me a Catholic, if not good.

But it was my own "Catholicity" that I was beginning
to doubt, the more so after a further heavy blow: the
signing of the Reich Concordat with the Vatican engi-
neered by von Papen and Monsignor Kaas. After the
seizure of power, the Reichstag fire, and the March
election, it was, incredibly, the Vatican that accorded
the Nazis their first major international recognition.
Some members of our family—myself among them—
seriously considered leaving the church, but that had
become so fashionable among all those Germans who
couldn't wait to join the Nazi Party after the March
1933 election that we didn't, since it might have been
misconstrued as homage to the Nazis. That didn't
exempt us from considerable crises, both existential
and political, yet in the midst of that time of crisis, I
took part in a procession, strutting proudly along as I
carried a great flag (white with an enormous blue ⚑),
accepting as an honor the occasional, not general,

mockery of the spectators. I don't even remember in what procession or what group I was "performing"; all I can be sure of is the pride, the flag, and the recollection of one particular bunch of mockers on St. Apern-Strasse. It is quite possible that I was still a member of that Marian fellowship to which I had so enthusiastically belonged: those weekend outings, "leaving gray city walls behind," those amateur theatricals, puppet shows, hiking over hill and dale, the singing, pennants, campfires! I left the fellowship when it brought in a paramilitary drill that even included "wheeling" on almost a company scale. And during that time of crisis I agreed to help out the parish of St. Maternus by taking over the distribution of the *Junge Front*, the last weekly of Catholic youth until its brave demise. I was recruited for this job by Otto Vieth over streusel cake and ersatz coffee in the garden of St. Vincent's Hospital in Cologne-Nippes. The job was also a source of income: the ten pfennigs paid for each copy of the *Junge Front* didn't have to be turned in until the following week and helped us over many a straitened weekend.

At the time there was also a theory, almost officially sanctioned by the church, that one should join the Nazi organizations in order to "Christianize them from within"—whatever that may have meant, for to this day no one seems to know what "Christianization" consists of. A considerable number—among them our

principal, I believe—acted on this theory, and after
the war many of them, left in the lurch in the denazifi-
cation process, had to pay for it.

Although I had long since ceased to be "organized,"
I still ostentatiously wore the ⚡ insignia on my lapel
and more than once had to take abuse from an older
student who, not surprisingly, had been a particularly
enthusiastic member of the Catholic youth movement.
That was the extent of what I had to put up with in
school. I had no trouble with my classmates; they had
known me and I them for five or six years; there were
arguments but no attempts at conversion. Some disap-
proved of my occasional flippant remarks about Hitler
and other Nazi bigwigs, but none of them, not even the
S.S. member, would ever, I believe, have dreamed of
denouncing me. I felt no resentment, not even toward
the teachers. We still thought it possible that the Nazis
wouldn't last; sometimes we'd even laugh in anticipa-
tion of further opportunistic contortions of the "bourgeoisie" *when* . . . But *who* would then take over none
of us tried to predict.

I kept up my friendships with several of my classmates
even after graduation (although I avoided that S.S.
fellow: in the three years preceding graduation I
doubt if I exchanged more than two sentences with
him). We pored over our homework together, and I

tried to help some of them over that strange German math trauma, with the zeal of the convert: not long before, my brother Alfred had cured me of this trauma by systematically and patiently "probing back" to my basic knowledge, discovering gaps, closing them, and thus giving me a firm foundation. That had led us to such an enthusiasm for math that we spent weeks trying to discover a method of trisecting the angle, and sometimes we felt so close to the solution that we spoke only in whispers. The "furnished gentleman" living in the next room had a degree in engineering, which might have enabled him to appropriate our discovery.

Yes, I pored over textbooks with them, crammed for math and Latin (another of those traumatic subjects that fortunately never developed into a trauma for me). Sometimes we spent the evening in my father's office in the rear courtyard of the building at 28 Vondel-Strasse. Money being scarce and cigarettes and tobacco expensive, we would buy the very cheapest kind of cigars (five pfennigs each), cut them up with a razor blade, and roll them into cigarettes. (Today I am sure we were suffering from an economic delusion.) The tiny office building was seductively cozy, built entirely of wood, something between a log cabin and a shed. It contained fine, solidly built closets, with sliding doors of green glass, for the storage of metal fittings and drawings: little neo-Gothic turrets, miniature columns, flowers, figures of saints; designs for

confessionals, pulpits, altars and communion benches,
furniture; and there was also an old copying press
from pre–World War I days, and a few remaining
cartons of light bulbs for bayonet sockets, although we
had shot hundreds of them to pieces in the garden on
Kreuznacher-Strasse. Green desk lamps, a big table
with a green linoleum top; slabs of glue, tools. When
it came to gluing, the generational conflict between my
father and my brother Alois was concentrated on the
"barbaric, revolutionary" invention of cold glue,
which my father didn't trust, while my brother demon-
strated its reliability; but my father insisted on hot,
boiled glue, the way it had to be prepared in the glue
pot, with constant stirring, from the honey-colored
slabs. There was no lack of other conflicts, but they
have no place here.

5

YES, also school, but first, in that horror-year of
1933 after Hitler's seizure of power, the Reichstag fire,
terror, the March election, and the body blow of the
Reich Concordat, something happened that caused
even the middle classes of Cologne to tremble. In
July—the Concordat had been completed but not yet

signed—the trial took place in Cologne of seventeen members of the Red Front Fighters' League, for murder in two cases, attempted murder in one: the murders of Storm Troopers Winterberg and Spangenberg, who had just recently converted from the Communist Party to the Nazis. But seventeen murderers? Nobody believed that, nor was it ever established who had actually shot the two men. The trial began in July; in September, seven of the seventeen accused were condemned to death, and on November 3 they were beheaded with an ax. All pleas for mercy had been rejected. There was no pardon. Göring, Minister-President of Prussia, declared: "As a result of these incidents I have decided not to wait another day but to intervene with an iron fist. In future anyone who lays violent hands on a representative of the National Socialist movement or a representative of the State must realize that he will lose his life in short order."

The reason for my placing that event one year later, in the fall of 1934, may have something to do with June 30, 1934, that ultimate brutal step to the seizure of total power. That day has remained in my memory as a crucial signal—perhaps because the time up until June 30 seemed relatively quiet to me. Nowadays I often think of those seven young Communists in view of the miserably embarrassing palaver over recognition of the resistance group known as the Edelweiss pirates.

One thing I do know, even if the date has shifted in my memory: on the day of the executions, shock hung over Cologne, fear and shock, the kind that before a thunderstorm makes birds flutter up into the sky and seek shelter. It became quiet, quieter; I no longer made flippant remarks about Hitler, except at home, and even there not in everyone's presence.

One of the executed men, the youngest, aged nineteen, wrote poems in his death cell. The place where they were written, the fate of the author, lift those lines far beyond what one might patronizingly call "touching," which is why, for fear of diminishing their deadly seriousness, I won't quote them. The poems, written by a Red Front fighter, reveal the "Italian" nature of Cologne Communism (as it then was). In one poem he gives thanks for the candles lighted for him in church, admitting that he was present at the deed and declaring that he did not commit murder; at the end of the poem he thanks his friend, a Red Front fighter, for having prayed with him at night—and asks that the Lord's Prayer be said at his grave.

For Göring, whose soldier-emperor fantasies seemed, in the observations of many of his contemporaries, comical if not almost endearing—for that robber, that murderer, that bloodthirsty fool, I and many other Cologne schoolkids were soon lining the streets. During those few hours in Cologne, he changed uniforms three if not four times. It surprises me that some

waggish moviemaker has not yet discovered *this* character: that masklike face with its glittering morphine
addict's eyes, that "mighty hunter before the Lord,"
that inflated Nimrod, known later as "Herr Meyer"—
surely the perfect subject for a movie farce! As it was,
his scenes with Dimitroff, the Bulgarian Communist,
during the Reichstag fire trial did much to enhance our
considerable political amusement. At the time when
the executions were announced, however, the entire
city trembled under that bloody fist—it's possible, of
course, that I was crediting the whole city with my own
horror.

6

SCHOOL? Oh yes, that too. Soon I had reached that
level of education known as "lower school-leaving
certificate." For serious economic reasons my family
considered taking me out of school and putting me to
work as an apprentice. One possibility being considered was land surveying ("You'll always be out in
the fresh air"—my aversion to fug being well known
—"besides, it's a nice way of earning a living, what
with math and all that, which you're so fond of").
Another suggestion: a commercial apprenticeship with
a coffee wholesaler on (I forget whether Grosse or
Kleine) Witsch-Gasse, where a friend of ours had some

connections. Land surveyor: that really didn't sound
too bad, and for a few hours I wavered, until I realized
that it would mean a more or less bureaucratic occupation: that smelled of being forcibly organized. Yet,
even today, when I drive through the countryside and
see land surveyors at work with their instruments and
measuring rods, I sometimes indulge in the fancy that
I might have become one of them; the office of the
coffee wholesaler on (Grosse or Kleine) Witsch-Gasse,
when in later years I happened to pass by it, would
provoke a strangely gentle nostalgia in me: that *would
have been*, that *might have been:* although I was firmly
resolved to become a writer, the detour via land
surveying and the coffee business wouldn't have been
any worse than other roundabout routes I subsequently
took. (It is only now that I can appreciate, compre-
hend, how utterly horrified my family must have been
when, between quitting my bookseller's apprenticeship
and starting my stint in the Labor Service, between
February and November 1938, when I was not yet
twenty-one—and in the very midst of firmly entrenched
Nazi terror—I actually set out to be a free-lance
writer.)

The decision to take me out of school was dropped,
as the result of my own strenuous objections and those
of my older brothers and sisters. Employment of any
kind inexorably meant being organized, and that was
a condition I had always avoided and intended to go

on avoiding. I enjoyed studying but wasn't that keen on school, started being bored for long periods of time, and might actually have dropped out if it hadn't been for the Nazis. But I knew, and was fully aware of the fact: school, *that* school at any rate, was the best hiding place I could find, and so, strictly speaking, I have the Nazis to thank for my graduation. Perhaps that is why I wasn't interested in the graduation ceremonies or in my certificate, submitting it unread when I later applied for a job as an apprentice.

From then on, after having acquired "my lower school-leaving certificate," I began to orchestrate the school for my own ends. Three more years to graduation, how many more years to war—perhaps less than three? And I was too much of a coward to risk becoming a conscientious objector. That much I knew: the mute, stony-faced men released from concentration camps, the idea of possible torture—no, I didn't have the guts. To escape the war, no matter where, was simply beyond the realm of the imagination. (Not long ago we were asked by Frank G., aged thirty-seven, born in the last year but one of the war, why we hadn't emigrated, and we found it hard to explain that such an idea was simply beyond the realm of our imagination: it was as if someone had asked why I hadn't ordered a taxi to the moon. Of course we knew that people had emigrated: Jewish friends—didn't I regularly read *Der Stürmer* in the display box on Severin-

Strasse?—and even a man like Brüning, but *us?*
Where to and in what capacity? We were, in a funny
way, a Catholic family that happened to be against the
Nazis; but all that is hindsight. At the time it was simply way beyond our thoughts. Later I did very briefly
consider, and reject, a variation of emigration: deser-
tion to a foreign army. You won't be *that* welcome over
there, I thought, so I deserted in the other direction—
to my home.)

That same year, 1934, all those who had believed that
Hitler wouldn't last long were refuted: June 30 swept
all those hopes away, a summer day rife with rumors,
tensions, and a strange, indefinable admixture of
euphoria. Surely that couldn't be true: that so many
leading Nazis were criminals and even homosexuals?
(That Röhm was one we knew, of course: the slogan
"Wash your asses, Storm Troopers, Röhm's coming!"
had been appearing on the walls of buildings before
and even after 1933.) When all was said and done,
the openness with which dirty linen was now being
washed in public was truly amazing. Perhaps it was a
sign of weakness. Within a few hours we realized the
obvious: it was a sign of strength, and at long last we
knew the meaning of a Party purge.

We still had no radio, and that day I was all over
the place on my bike, for once (why "for once" will be

explained—patience!) even in the center of town, at
the Heumarkt, the Neumarkt, the cathedral, the railway station. Something was in the air, people were
talking in whispers and undertones, full of hope—
until at last Hitler spoke and the "special editions"
appeared on the streets. I bought one and when I got
home took the little bundle of Alva cigarette cards out
of my desk drawer, the series showing all the promi-
nent Nazis. I sorted out all those who had been shot: it
was a tidy little pile. The faces that remain in my
memory are those of Heines and Röhm.

That was—and we were aware of it—not merely
the final seizure of power but also the ultimate test of
power, the final unmasking of von Papen and Hindenburg. Klausener, Jung, and Schleicher were among the
murdered, and apparently no one said a word, at least
not audibly; no one said a word, nothing happened. It
was the dawn of the eternity of Nazism. Did the middle classes, the Nationalists, know what was happen-
ing, the pass they had come to? I am afraid they still
don't know: one of the most ludicrous days in German
history, the day of Potsdam, March 21, 1933, when
Hindenburg handed Germany over to a gentleman in a
tailcoat, must have blinded them all.

That same year, right after June 30, according to
a decree that had been made before June 30, the
weekly National Youth Day was introduced; it didn't
become law—that, I believe, didn't happen until 1939;

it was merely *decreed*. Just try to imagine the situation: a state in which a character, a jerk, like Baldur
von Schirach, was in control of the entire youth of the
country! We knew, although meanwhile it appears to
have been forgotten, that he was a poet: a German poet
in control of German youth! From among his many
poems there was one line we knew by heart, and we
would hum and recite it *sotto voce:* "I was a leaf so
free, searching for my tree." (Must I at this point
come to the aid of praiseworthy lyric interpretation
and explain who the leaf so free was and who the tree?
I will if you like!) Sometime before 1933, when the
University of Cologne was still on Claudius-Strasse,
only a minute away from us, Schirach had been beaten
up by "leftist students" after a poetry reading. So it
was this jerk of a Schirach who had complete control
over German youth, and German parents allowed him
to hold sway over their sons and daughters.

Of the approximately two hundred boys at our school
there were three who on National Youth Day were not
exempted from classes to allow them to be "on duty."
Being "on duty" probably meant participating in some
sort of paramilitary sports: I don't know exactly, I
never asked the other boys about it, not even those I
did my homework with. We talked about movies and
girls, not about politics, and when one of them tried

to raise the subject I shut up. I was scared, whereas at home I could talk, even if one of them was present: surely no one would dare denounce our family. Today I sometimes think that some relatively high Nazi, who never revealed himself, must have "held his hand over our family."

So on Saturdays (Saturday being a regular school day) we three, Bollig, Koch, and myself, had to go to school and, under the supervision of a teacher, who obviously found it a bore and a nuisance (I suppose otherwise he would have had the day off), tidy up the school library. Every Saturday for three years we three tidied up that tiny little library housed in a room next to what used to be the caretaker's quarters. Not one title, not one author, not one book that I held in my hand has remained in my memory. No, I certainly didn't suffer, and I met with no difficulty whatever, not the slightest. I assume that after two Saturdays there was nothing left to tidy in what was from the start a tidy library; so we would smoke cigarettes (if we had any), drink school cocoa, go out for some ice cream, kill time. Usually the teacher in charge left us to our own devices from ten o'clock on and went home or to a café, putting Mirgeler the caretaker in charge, who in turn let us off by eleven o'clock at the latest.

Mirgeler was a kind, gentle person, one of the few disabled veterans who didn't talk about his war experiences. One could feel he was on our side, not explicitly—that would have been too dangerous and we didn't expect it of him. And of course one could always be sick on Saturday or get sick. With Mirgeler and several of the teachers, there was no need for explicitness, the expression on their faces was enough. For some of the teachers, as well as for Mirgeler, we were, at least after the occupation of the Rhineland in 1936, *morituri*, and that softened many a severe reprimand or punishment that would have been deserved in "normal times." If I were to say that, with the introduction of Schirach's National Youth Day, the pressure was increased, it would be an exaggeration. From time to time—not often, later not at all—we were summoned to the principal, one by one, and he would try to persuade us to join the Hitler Youth or, later, the Storm Troopers. He did not really press us, it was more of a plea, alluding, not very convincingly, to its being "for our own good." Obviously he was running into trouble, we three were lousing up the statistics. Quite clearly he didn't feel at ease on these occasions, and his pleas were in vain: we remained adamant all the time we were in school. I have always wondered why no personal friendships developed among us three. They didn't. Moreover, one or another of us was always absent those Saturdays, sometimes two of us or even all three. Eventually there was hardly so much as a pretense of checking up on that strange "library work."

The pleas in the principal's arguments were more dangerous than threats would have been, for—and I'm sorry to say he probably never discovered this—I rather liked him. He was gentler than he sometimes pretended or had to pretend to be, the type of person known as strict but fair, yet easily moved to tears: a good history teacher, and, besides Latin and math, history was one of my favorite and deliberately orchestrated courses. It is he whom I have to thank for my early insight into the nature of colonialism as exemplified by the Roman Empire; insight into the parasitic bribed-vote existence of the rabble of ancient Rome. He was probably what today I would call "blinded" by Hindenburg, a fatal attribute of many decent Germans: patriotic, not nationalistic, certainly not Nazist, but very much the veteran, fond of telling us about tight situations in trench warfare where as a young officer he had been wounded in the head; yet also Catholic, a Rhinelander with a gentle "von" to his name.

When the first former student of our school was killed in the Spanish Civil War, a member of the Condor Legion who was shot down—possibly over Guernica—he organized a memorial service and, with tears in his eyes, made a moving speech. I didn't feel comfortable at this service, didn't want to share his emotion although I had known the dead man, who had been a classmate of my brother's. Today I interpret

that vague feeling of discomfort as follows: school
prepared us not for life but for death. Year after year,
German high school graduates were being prepared
for death. Was dying for the Fatherland the supreme
merit? To put it flippantly: at that service one might
have gained the impression that our principal was sad
at *not* having been killed at Langemarck. I know that
sounds harsh, but I am not being unfair to a dead
man: in the final analysis, the fatal role played by
those highly educated, unquestionably decent German
high school teachers led to Stalingrad and made
Auschwitz possible: that Hindenburg blindness. I can't
swear to the degree of truth contained in the following
supposition: it has been said that the principal was
told by high, if not the highest, clerics to join the Nazi
Party, "in order to salvage what could be salvaged."
(As we have since discovered, there was nothing to be
salvaged; and I also know that it is easy enough to say
that with hindsight.) We discussed the problem with
our friends, found the idea not dishonorable but fool-
ish. However, we didn't withdraw our friendship from
those who were persuaded by the argument.

Incidentally, even our own family didn't withstand
the pressure: when the *Kölnische Volkszeitung* and
the *Rhein-Mainische Zeitung* ceased publication, we too
subscribed to the *Westdeutsche Beobachter* and got
mad at the ingenious articles by the Catholic author
Heinz Steguweit. ("A swastika, a lovely sight, before

which kneels Heinz Steguweit.") Following the insistent "advice" of our block warden, we too acquired a swastika flag after 1936, albeit a small one: on days when displaying the flag was compulsory, sentiments could *also* be deduced from the size of the flags.

By that time my father, insofar as he received any orders at all, had almost ceased working for churches and monasteries; almost all his orders were now government ones. And when those orders became even scarcer, he was urged to have at least one member of his family join a Nazi organization. A kind of family council was called, and my brother Alois became the victim of its decision, since, after some miserable receivership proceedings, he was officially the owner of the business. He was elected by the family to join the Storm Troopers. (To the end of his days he bore a grudge against us for this, and he was right: we should at least have drawn lots.) Of all the members of our family, he was the worst suited for that mimicry: the person least suited for a uniform I have ever known, and he *suffered*, he really suffered from those mob parades and route marches. I don't know how often he actually took part in those route marches—certainly not more than three times. Nor do I remember how often I went to see his platoon leader, a very recently converted former Communist who lived in a tiny attic above Tappert's drugstore at the corner of Bonner-Strasse and Roland-Strasse. There, on behalf of my brother, I would bribe that character—whom I remember as being depraved but not unfriendly—with a pack of ten R6 cigarettes, available in those days in nice-looking, flat, red packs, positively luxurious, to list my permanently absent brother as present. He did so, and among our flippant variations of the Rosary decades we included the words: "Thou who hast joined the Storm Troopers for our sakes." And the "Full is Her right hand of gifts" was changed to: "Full is thy right hand of R6's."

7

Yes, school. I had no problems, either educational or political; no one bothered me anymore. It was taken for granted that I must have passing grades; we couldn't afford for me to fail a year, yet the idea was tempting: it would have extended the duration of my hiding place by a year provided that . . . it must not be forgotten that we were moving toward war, it was a matter not of *après nous* but *avant nous le déluge*. I was determined not to learn for dying, which for many if not all German high school graduates had been preached as the highest goal in life. So in life I was learning for school, and in school—as will be shown— a few things for living. I concentrated entirely on the

subjects I liked: Greek, Latin, math, history, studying
for these subjects even when I didn't go to school. I
enjoyed translating a Latin text for my own pleasure,
with no direct benefit. In later years I sometimes stayed
home to continue working by myself on Sophocles'
Antigone, because the slow rate of progress in school
made me impatient. In the other subjects I did enough
not to slip below a C and, if it happened to suit me,
turned up for tests.

If I pushed things too far, the principal would
phone my mother and ask whether I was really that
sick. I had an almost unshakable, permanent alibi,
known in those days as chronic sinus infection, which
actually did bother me for years, causing headache
and nausea whenever I attempted to bend down. Today
I sometimes think that condition was Nazi-induced (let
doctors and psychologists mull that one over: I am
sure there are such things as politically- or system-
induced illnesses). There was one advantage to that
condition: it released me from gym, which I hated.
Yes, I admit it: I disliked gym, it always smelled of
male sweat, of strenuous efforts, so the illness, even
when I suffered no attacks for months on end, suited
me down to the ground. (Oh those heat lamps, those
hot camomile douches!) What I did miss, though, was
track and field, and games—and my beloved streets of
Cologne. On one or two occasions during my roamings,
one of those Nazi hordes happened to come marching

around the corner, and everyone ran to the curb to raise their right arms while I just barely managed to duck into a doorway. The horror lay deep (it still does!), and even the remotest possibility of such a horde suddenly turning up soured me toward the streets of Cologne.

It was a kind of banishment, so from being a pedestrian I became a cyclist, taking refuge in distant suburbs in the "green belt," riding up and down along the Rhine between Niehl and Rodenkirchen, across to Deutz. I came to love cycling, and cycling became my sole regular sport. I had enjoyed field sports (as for gym, Oh, that ludicrous virile earnestness!)—soccer and other games (including rounders), track and field: all that came to an end after the introduction of National Youth Day. The two afternoon periods known officially as "Games" came to an end; how often we had extended them far beyond the set time, on summer afternoons on the Poll Meadows, and had played many of those games outside of school hours, rounders especially. Meanwhile it was *verboten* to pursue "unorganized" sports. My brother Alois was once briefly taken into custody when he went off with a few boys from the parish to play soccer on the Poll Meadows: it wasn't anything ominous, merely a *sign*, and meant, as he was firmly told, as a warning.

So cycling became my only sport. I explored unfamiliar suburbs, rode up or down beside the Rhine to quiet places along the banks, and I read (yes, Hölderlin too). With repair kit, pump, and a carbide lamp, I was independent—almost, with only a few books on the carrier and a bit of tobacco in my pocket, almost a "traveller without luggage." And I could also go for a swim: totalitarianism was not yet quite complete.

8

YES, school too. At times I even obtained quite good grades in German literature. Not that I've retained much from my reading of it: there are only a few authors I can still call to mind, one of them by the name of Adolf Hitler, author of *Mein Kampf*, compulsory reading. Our teacher, Mr. Schmitz, a man of penetrating, witty, dry irony (for some authors a little *too* dry!), used the hallowed texts of Adolf Hitler the writer to demonstrate the importance of concise expression, known also as brevity. This meant we had to take four or five pages from *Mein Kampf* and reduce them to two, if possible one and a half: "condense" that unspeakable, badly convoluted German (there also exists some very nicely convoluted German!). Think what that meant: "condensing" the Führer's texts! Taking that kind of German apart and tightening it up appealed to me. So I read *Mein Kampf* minutely, which, again, didn't increase my respect for the Nazis by one iota. Just the same, I can thank Adolf Hitler the writer for a few badly needed B's in German literature; perhaps also—something else I learned in school for my life—for some qualification to be a publisher's reader and a liking for brevity. To this day I am surprised that no one noted the lack of respect implied in the process of "condensing" the Führer's texts, and it was many years before I realized this myself, realized all the implications of such an assignment. And it was a great many years later, when my former teacher Karl Schmitz, plagued by terrible headaches, would sometimes come to see us on Schiller-Strasse, after 1945, for a cup of black market coffee, that I could show him my respect and gratitude.

Another author, but one I cannot thank for good grades, was a certain Hanns Johst, whose play *Schlageter* we had not only to read but see performed: every school in Cologne was virtually herded through the theater, and, if I remember rightly, there were even morning performances. My impression: a very weak play. The hero, who was executed by the French in the occupied Rhineland in 1923 for sabotage, impressed me neither as a Catholic nor as a saboteur; on the other hand, he wasn't weak enough to impress me as an anti-hero.

For some of my good grades in German literature (which were rare enough), I have Jeremias Gotthelf to thank. No longer under Schmitz, we made a thorough study of those nineteenth-century rustic novels *Uli the Plowboy* and *Uli the Tenant Farmer* and wrote essays on them. No doubt about it, Vreneli the maid appealed to me more than Uli did. I filled pages and pages with Vreneli's generosity of spirit as compared to Uli's timid pettiness, thinking what men often think: that girl was too good for him! And I elaborated (may God and Gotthelf forgive me!) on the differences between the two being "milieu-conditioned."

I presume that Gotthelf found his way into the curriculum because some Nazi "blood and soil" strategist believed that through him we would be brought closer to peasant emotions, thoughts, and behavior. Our study of Gotthelf culminated in a final essay entitled "City and Land, Hand in Hand" (a popular Nazi slogan). In this essay I made an impassioned plea for the city, boldly (and erroneously, as I have long since realized) declaring Vreneli to have been an urban type. (It would be worth while making a study someday of the stupid mistakes and superficial ideological assumptions that allow certain books to be "permitted" or to "slip through" under dictatorships, as, for instance, Evelyn Waugh, whom we promptly took to be a woman, or Bloy and Bernanos, whose anticlericalism was thoroughly misinterpreted.)

9

YES, school too. Times got colder, tougher, even financially, and we were moving toward the war. Much remained: the loyalty of my parents and my brothers and sisters, of friends, even those who had long since joined Nazi organizations. There remained the irreplaceable, almost sacred bicycle, that swift vehicle of mobility, an escape-vehicle light of build, worthy of many a paean and, as I found out by 1945, the only reliable and the most valuable mechanical means of locomotion. Think of everything an automobile requires! How clumsy it actually is, dependent on a thousand minor factors, to say nothing of fuel, of roads: on a bicycle a person can go anywhere. And let us not forget: the Vietnam war was won on bicycles against tanks and planes. Repair kit, pump, lamp— easy to carry, almost no luggage at all. And how about all the things you can, if you have to, hang onto a bike or load onto it?

The sinus condition remained too, right through my stint with the glorious Labor Service and the equally glorious Army; but the moment I became a prisoner of war, in that strange state of simultaneous liberation and imprisonment, and in the years after the war and up to this very day: gone without a trace!

Was it really Nazi-induced? It may well have been, for I was *also* allergic to the Nazis.

While still living on Maternus-Strasse, we used to walk across the grim-looking South Bridge, along the Rhine past Poll, through Poll, between wheat fields fragrant with summer, on dusty field paths, the water tower as a landmark ahead of us, toward the fortifications where my brother Alfred was doing his "voluntary" labor service. (Completion of this "voluntary" labor service happened to be "merely" a requirement for entering university.) Those dim, dank casemates built in the 1880's, from which—contrary to expectations since my brother wasn't yet eligible to leave camp— we asked for him to be summoned! He would emerge looking to me like a convict, thoroughly cowed. As a high school graduate he was automatically an "intellectual" and, as such, had to take a lot of abuse and do the heaviest work. At the camp entrance stood two —always the same two—young yet already worn-out whores, pathetic creatures who for a pittance would lie down in the bushes with anyone who managed to bribe or persuade the sentry. That conglomeration of underground, damp, dismal Wilhelminian fortifications, the smell, the depressing atmosphere, the two whores who weren't even minimally "dolled up" (they were the only ones available for miles around)—all of that was anything but uplifting. We would take along a few cigarettes, chat dejectedly for a while, conscious of the barbarity of visits in or outside any barracks. (Oh, Lili Marleen, don't you know we never stood "by the lantern?" Who would ever choose to stand with a girl, let alone *his* girl, by the lantern outside "the heavy door?" In the darkest corner along the wall, that's where we stood—and it wasn't sweet either: out of your arms back into that stale, sweaty male atmosphere!) Depressed, we would wend our way home, along the railway embankment, the dust of summer on our lips, the smell of the wheat fields—I had it in my heart, my brain, my consciousness, that *foretaste*, which, only a few years later, turned out to be correct: I knew that I would be caught up in it, that I lacked the strength and the courage to elude the two uniforms in store for me.

We walked home, summer evening, water tower, railway embankment, wheat fields, the Rhine. Had they already started building the barracks in Poll-Porz that year? That rumor led to many an interrogation and arrest of those who were already claiming something that soon turned out to be true: barracks were being built there, although the Rhineland was still a demilitarized zone. Were the foundations already being laid at that time for the Cologne–Rodenkirchen autobahn bridge, that strategic opening toward the West?

Once again, and again: school, *too*, yes. With the two real Nazis among the teachers (both the loud-mouth, roughneck type), we had nothing to do, so I had no problems with my teachers, though they may have had some with me. Whenever a student tried to offset his miserable Greek or Latin with his uniform (which didn't happen very often), Mr. Bauer, whom I had as a teacher from the fourth to the twelfth grades, would catch my eye. There was no need for words between us; he was a democrat, a humanist, not even remotely obsessed with war. He pointed out how relevant to our own time was the element of parody in Greek comedy; sometimes he would talk about smoking cigars and drinking sherry; he overlooked impudence; and later he read Juvenal with us. Juvenal and Tacitus were his Latin favorites. (I saw Bauer one last time, in the late fall of 1944, from a moving hospital train: he was in a wheelchair on the station platform in Ahrweiler or Remagen.)

Problems with teachers? No. Even my problem with our teacher of religion subsided. I didn't even have one with our gym teacher: although I was "exempt from gym" (hence, in the eyes of a gym teacher, almost asocial), he would sometimes invite me to his home or ask me to take part illicitly in a rounders match against another school. I wasn't a bad batter—it ran in the family, my two older brothers being practically rounders stars, and we had played a

lot on the meadows of the Vorgebirg Park. So there I
would be, illicitly hitting the ball beside Aachen Pond
or in Blücher Park in a game against one of the
Cologne high schools.

One thing I must make clear: I never thought of
myself as being better than my classmates, or even
"untainted," merely—oh, tiny "merely"!—alien,
everything going on outside of me seemed alien and
became more and more alien. Only my bike and my
truancy saved me from shutting myself away in my
room, yet now I was spending more time there, translating Latin or Greek texts for my own pleasure, and,
long before I reached eighteen, I must have been well
on the way to turning from an outsider into an eccentric. My bike wasn't my only salvation; there were also
a few girls.

However, my progress was far from reassuring.
My family, our friends, were justifiably worried, and
more and more often the question was asked: "What's
to become of the boy?" My brothers and sisters all
either had a profession or were clearly on the road to
one: schoolteacher, bookkeeper, cabinetmaker, theology student. Theology? Not so farfetched, and it would
have offered an escape, but within minutes I had decided and declared that theology was not for me. As a
study it had its attractions, but in those days theology
and the priesthood were synonymous, and to that there
was an obstacle that I would like to define as dis-

creetly as possible: the beauties and other charms—
profound and less profound—of the female sex were
no secret to me, and I was of no mind to renounce
them. Celibacy—what a horrifying word that was! To
start out by contemplating double moral standards was
beyond all consideration, and in those days such a
thing as laicization (but then why become a priest if
you are already speculating about laicization?) was
as unimaginable as a trip to the moon. And finally:
vestigia terrebant. The traces were frightening. I knew
of cases of entanglements with family and friends, of
those who had "tripped," "stumbled," "slipped,"
"fallen"; and many a one essaying a trip to the moon
had landed flat on his face.

My father had done a lot of work for churches and
monasteries, and his knowledge of that world, which
he did not withhold from us, was more than adequate;
probably it explained why he had strictly forbidden us
to act as altar boys (an activity, by the way, that had
never even remotely appealed to me). And then, of
course, there was—an option that was vigorously discussed, there being plenty of theology students around
—the path of "sublimation," but I hadn't the slightest
desire to sublimate *that.*

10

THE VIEW IS occasionally expressed that, after January 30, 1933, the day of Hitler's seizure of power, some kind of economic miracle took place. However, as far as our family is concerned, I cannot affirm this. The fact of my brother's having joined the Storm Troopers availed us nothing (variation of the Rosary line: "Thou who hast joined the Storm Troopers for our sakes in vain"). We were worse off than before 1933, and that can't have been due entirely to "political unreliability." My father had many well-disposed, old friends in government positions. Nevertheless, our most time-consuming and laborious occupation continued to be: opening up new credit for groceries or paying off old accounts so we could buy on credit again, and then the never-ending burden of: the rent.

To this day I don't know what we lived on. How? To say we lived "from hand to mouth" would be euphemistic. There is no doubt—and I suggest the political economists cudgel their brains before they shake their heads—that we lived *beyond* and *below* our means. One thing is verifiable: we survived, so those years were a kind of survival training. If there were any films, data, or bookkeeping relative to that time, I would gladly study them in order to discover

how, but there are no records: there were merely re-
peated family councils where lists were drawn up,
budgets decided upon, and pocket money—according
to age and sex ("But the girls need stockings!")—was
entered in my father's little black notebooks. All that
might be called quite "literary." But as for being an
economic miracle, far from it. There were frequent
quotations from Dickens, especially Mr. Micawber in
David Copperfield, who, as we know, was a mathematical wizard, a financial genius—although unrecog-
nized—able to calculate to the last penny precisely how
one rose to affluence, descended to poverty—and who
was forever landing in the debtors' prison. My father
was in no sense a Mr. Micawber: he was serious and
conscientious, desperate too, with a certain inclination
to "escape into the never-never," preferring to live beyond rather than below his means.

And so in 1936 we moved again—for the third
time in six years. It was the last time my parents moved
house, the bombs took care of the rest; it was an
"escape into the never-never," into a somewhat more
expensive area, to Karolinger-Ring, into an apartment
that had been built thirty years earlier as "high-style
accommodation." Having had two "furnished gentlemen" on Ubier-Ring and one on Maternus-Strasse, we
now permitted ourselves the luxury (might as well go
down in style!) of having none at all. In view of our
financial situation, which was anything but improved,

that move was certainly not logical, but it was con-
sistent. We had the mad, perhaps even criminal, desire
to *live* and to survive. Somehow we managed.

School? Yes. Studying was still important to me,
even if I did my best to avoid school. I pored over
math books and Latin texts, and there was one subject
in which my desire to learn, indeed my craving for
knowledge, was not satisfied in school: geography. I
loved atlases, at times collected them, tried to find out
how and *on what* people lived *where*. I suppose that's
called economic geography. I hunted through ency-
clopedias and—somehow—got hold of reading material. In my father's library (which, on the whole, I
despised), I found a multivolume anthropological work
by a missionary that I devoured in my search for accounts of expeditions—all this on the side, of course.

Also on the side I became "secretary" to Chaplain
Paul Heinen of St. Maternus Church. I set up a filing
system for him, took care of some of his correspon-
dence, and from time to time he would give me a coin
or two from his pittance of a salary. It wasn't much
more than a "game" and an escape: the deluge was not
yet behind us, it still lay ahead. At some point in 1936
I saw Heinen for the last time, ran into him on Severin-
Strasse. I was surprised at his haste, the way he could
barely wait to say good-bye. A few days later I learned
that on that very day he had been on his way out of the
country, to emigrate via Holland to America. I believe

he must have been too friendly with (then still Chaplain) Rossaint. I never heard any details.

11

MATERIAL SURVIVAL took priority over political survival. There were grim days, weeks, and months; there were many pleasures and friends. There were the cheap, magnificent concerts in Gürzenich Hall, surprisingly bold lectures at the Catholic Academic League initiated by the priest Robert Grosche. There were movies, and at night, after dark, when you no longer had to worry about the Nazi hordes, you could go for a carefree walk, perhaps even with a girl. Cologne was still a livable city. And within a short time there appeared on the scene that special girl, called Annemarie. But that would take me too far beyond the time I am describing, and if I were to go beyond that period—back long before 1933, if possible as far back as 1750, and forward beyond 1937, perhaps up to 1981—if I were to go beyond that period, it would lead to an enormous family tome: interesting perhaps, as interesting as any family history, but no more interesting than that. So I will limit myself to the period in question, as far as possible to its *externals*, revealing only those internal goings-on that form part

of, or arise from, the externals. Not even a hint, there-
fore, of the tensions, conflicts, problems, and semi-
tragedies; and if I have a stab at those four years and
some gaiety should show up here and there, it's nothing
but the truth. However, that gaiety was often of the
desperate kind seen in some medieval paintings, where
the laughter of the redeemed is sometimes akin to the
expression on the faces of the damned.

So somehow we managed, and after each move not
only our relatives and friends but also the bailiff and
the beggars were quick to discover our new address:
my mother never sent anyone away, and she had an
unruffled way of neither regarding bailiffs as enemies
nor treating them as such. As a result, we received
much good advice from them, and the pawnshop remained a familiar place to us. I can't say it was a good
time. We were both depressed and reckless, not the
slightest bit sensible. At the very moment when we
could least afford it, we would go out to a restaurant
for a meal. We would invite "furnished gentlemen,"
as long as we had any, for a game of cards, slyly in-
tending to win twenty pfennigs for a pack of Alvas or
Ecksteins, until we found to our amusement that they
had similar plans, so we would pool our resources and
enjoy a smoke together.

Every opportunity to make money was seized on;
the worst catastrophe of all was an attempt we made
to earn some, perhaps even acquire wealth, by address-

ing envelopes. We did own a typewriter, the one I later used to type my first short stories, influenced by Dostoievski, later by Bloy. (But I also wrote a novel, by hand, somewhat to the surprise of my future wife because the "hero" had two women.) The enterprise ended in disaster. Our employer, who was unemployed, also hoped to get rich with homemade birch rods for St. Nicholas to use on naughty boys. Not only did he expect us to type the addresses: we also had to pick them out of a telephone directory and supply the stationery. Question: who needs birch rods for St. Nicholas? Bakeries, pastry shops, grocery stores—a laborious job. Eventually it turned out that our employer was even worse off than we were—I don't know whether he ever unloaded any birch rods, and we never asked for more than the agreed wage, which came nowhere near covering our expenses.

And of course we helped in the workshop, if any help happened to be needed. With a wobbly two-wheeled handcart (which also did duty during our moves), we conveyed great stacks of new or repaired furniture to government offices. (Memories of Revenue Offices South, Old Town, and North! And the Regional Finance Administration on Wörth-Strasse, past which we sometimes stroll today on our way to the Rhine.) At night in the cashier's office of Revenue Office South (originally a Carthusian monastery secularized in 1806), we renovated the floor, which was said to date from Napoleonic times. We hoped to find coins, old ones if possbile, overlooking the fact that Carthusian monks of the eighteenth century weren't likely to have walked around with purses in their habits, and that latter-day visitors to the Revenue Office kept a tight grip on their pennies.

I was somewhat more successful in giving private lessons. The demand was small, the supply enormous: there was a plethora of unemployed teachers, B.A.'s, M.A.'s, and students, as well as sufficient *not* unemployed elementary and high school teachers anxious for some extra income. Immense supply, tiny demand, and that, of course, pushed down the prices (Oh, free market economy!). I found my first pupil through an advertisement, a nice boy whom I coached in Latin and math for fifty pfennigs an hour. I was more scared of his tests in school than he was; the result of those tests was the mark of success for which his parents were watching and waiting. I applied the method my brother had used with me: opening up gaps, closing gaps, and lo, he improved. An attempt at tutoring in French failed miserably, due to that boy's mother's excellent knowledge of French; she was quick to discover *my* gaps, graciously paid me off, and sent me home.

Before I dilate on the value of fifty pfennigs, let me merely point out that eight years later the hourly wage of an unskilled nursery-garden employee wasn't much higher—rather lower, in fact—than fifty

pfennigs, and that weekly unemployment assistance
for a family of three, including rental allowance,
amounted to less than seventeen marks. At the time I
am speaking of, my sister Mechthild, an unemployed
junior high school teacher, always loyal to the family,
was working as a governess in an aristocratic family
in Westphalia for thirty marks a month, of which she
sent home twenty-five. So a weekly extra income for a
totally "unskilled" person (who was later able to
increase his rate to seventy-five pfennigs an hour) of
four or five marks was, considering it was pure pocket
money, not to be sneezed at. It even permitted me to
open an account with a modern secondhand bookstore,
where I was allowed to pay in installments. I have no
intention here of playing off hard times against good
times, a ridiculous pastime for veterans, in my opinion.

Fifty pfennigs meant two or three secondhand
books—a Balzac for ten pfennigs and a Dostoievski
for twenty are what I still remember from the book bin
of a secondhand bookstore on Herzog-Strasse next door
to the Skala movie theater. Fifty pfennigs meant a
ticket to the cheapest seats in the movies plus three
cigarettes; it meant a piano recital on a student ticket
(Oh, Monique Haas!), two cups of coffee plus three
cigarettes, but also—and I sometimes treated my
mother and my sister Gertrud—four fresh rolls and
three or four slices of boiled ham, since, the Lord be
both praised and reproached, we always had an ap-

petite. My sister Gertrud would often reciprocate. And well-informed sources assured me that the minimum price for bought love in the back rooms of certain cafés in certain districts—provided by amateurs, I might add—had dropped to fifty pfennigs; of course only in "politically unreliable" areas—in a Germany that had just "awakened"!

12

I HAVE COME to the conclusion (at this late date!) that it really was living far, far beyond our means to let all the children in the family finish high school and then go on to university. Both my parents had only gone to elementary school: in their parents' eyes, secondary school was only for sons, and university was only considered if one of them wanted to study theology. (As a result, a boy with a passion and great talent for law became a not very happy priest, and a potential theologian became an atheistic high school teacher.) No doubt my parents had suffered more severely from this and other limitations than they admitted, and they wanted to see us children free, "unfolding freely."

The only reliable source of income was from time to time the "furnished gentlemen," but they didn't even cover the rent, and of the three small apartment

buildings my father had built to take care of his old
age (at the time he was already approaching seventy),
only one remained, an old tenement house, 28 Vondel-
Strasse, which also contained his workshop and office.
But that building was rarely in our own hands, and
then only for a short time; hardly ever was it *not* in
receivership. There were the inexorable municipal
taxes, the mortgage interest, the insurance premiums
—there was always someone bringing down an iron
fist upon us. What glorious times those were when the
building happened to be free and my sister Gertrud
went around collecting rents! Glorious but very brief
times, for soon that fist would come crashing down
again. Times didn't improve until later, after the period I am describing, when my brothers and sisters
were earning a bit of money.

Clever people will say—and rightly so—what
clever people were always saying at the time, that we
were *not sensible.* That's right, we weren't, for we were
even crazy enough to buy books and to read them: almost everything published by Jacob Hegener, as well
as Mauriac, Bernanos, and Bloy, plus Chesterton and
Dickens and Dostoievski, even old Weininger and
Claudel and Bergengruen (as long as he was available), even *Hammer Blows* by Lersch and, as I men-
tioned before, Evelyn Waugh and Timmermanns,
Ernest Hello, Reinhold Schneider, Gertrud von Le
Fort and, of course, Theodor Haecker. No, it wasn't

at all sensible, and sensible people borrowed the books from us, enjoyed dropping in at our place for discussions, and then sometimes a fractional Nazi, a quarter, a half, or even a whole Nazi, would come in for some abuse.

Those were lively sessions, yet at the same time a paralyzing pessimism lay over everything. We also played cards all night long, for money, although we knew that none of us would keep our winnings, and gaming debts piled up and were canceled, yet we went on playing as if in earnest. And I suppose it wasn't sensible either for a brother and sister of mine to work for my father—my brother in the workshop and my sister in the office—in a business where there was so little to do. Yet it was necessary for them to be there so as to keep the income derived from renting out the excellent machinery by the hour from getting into the hands of the bailiff. Things remained that tight until war broke out. (In wartime—and here I am going beyond 1937—money always flows easily, of course, and soon there was plenty to repair in Cologne. Wars also solve unemployment problems, a fact that is sometimes forgotten or suppressed when people talk about Hitler's "economic miracle." And wars also regulate the prices of cigarettes, which ultimately rose from one or one and a half pfennigs for the pale Dutch ones to eight hundred pfennigs for a single American cigarette.)

13

Yes, school too—I assure you, I'll soon get back to that. After all, I was still a pupil, a pupil of life so to speak, subject to despondency and recklessness, yet bound and determined not to become a pupil of death —if that could possibly be avoided. So, once again: somehow we managed. What was *vitally* important (I will forgo a few dozen anecdotes), and also a good schooling, was that our financial difficulties made us not humble but arrogant, not undemanding but demanding, and in some non-sensible way they made us sensible. No, we weren't expecting the pot of gold, but we did always expect more than we were entitled to or more than others considered we were entitled to ("others" being, for instance, the mathematical acrobats who worked out a subsistence minimum for us), and in the family we used to say: "Oliver Twist is asking for more." We developed an arrogance that assumed hysterical proportions, we made derogatory or blasphemous remarks about public institutions and personalities, and we needed no alcohol: words were enough.

After an evening of smearing and smirching, of more and more feverish, even frenetic, laughter at the expense of church, state, institutions, and personalities, my brother Alois, in a kind of hiatus of exhaustion, said something that then became a household phrase: "Now let's be Christians again!" And another expression for naïve, credulous, idealistic Nazis that we all hung onto was: "A blissful idiot." Those occasions were not only not comfortable, they were never harmonious; they were marked by a permanently dissonant loyalty. The three different elements blended in varying proportions in the individual members of the family, resulting in friction and tensions. Many a time, more than words flew through the air—bits and pieces, sometimes even quite sharp objects. Within each of us and among all of us, the elements clashed. Within each of us and among all of us, there was a class struggle. And then there were also periods influenced by alcohol, when we happened to have some money; on those occasions the products of the Hermanns distillery near the Severin Gate castle set the tone.

Yes, school. I didn't want the time I was spending there to be wasted, and my graduation certificate might survive—with me!—both the war and the Nazis, although it didn't look like it. The Nazis had become an eternity, the war was to become one, and war plus Nazis were a double eternity—yet I wanted to try to live beyond those four eternities (besides, for ten years my graduation certificate brought me the advantage of the flexible and useful occupational category of "student." But we aren't there yet).

. . .

Aside from school, Nazis, economic crises, there were other problems; for example, the ageless one of . . . *amore.* I tried—with what success I don't know—to keep all that a secret from the family, who were tearing their hair out anyway at the thought of my future —Oh my God, girls too? Or women even? There were many blows to come: after the introduction of conscription, the final blow was the occupation of the Rhineland, which we perceived as just that, an occupation. It may not have meant much, but, after all, the Rhineland had up to then, 1936, remained a demilitarized zone, and the last British occupation forces had taken their ceremonial departure only six years earlier. For my father, who, after Brüning's dismissal, had almost given up hope, the occupation of the Rhineland was the last straw, and now he too no longer doubted the imminence of war. Nazis disguised as Prussians, Prussians disguised as Nazis, in the Rhineland! We— I, at any rate—would have preferred to see the French —in spite of Schlageter!—or the British march in from the other side.

At this time my father would sometimes act out for our benefit again how, as a reservist en route to Verdun, he had caused himself to be carried off the train in Trier with a simulated attack of appendicitis —and it had worked: although he had to undergo an operation, he was never sent to the front. Final and

very impressive memory of Maternus-Strasse: an illegal meeting of the leaders of a Catholic young men's
association; the deep, ineradicable impression made
on me by Franz Steber: serious, determined, with no
illusions—and he paid dearly for that determination.
Shortly afterward, he was arrested, and during five
years of imprisonment by the Gestapo, his serious eye
trouble advanced to almost total blindness.

Less serious, but serious enough: shortly after our
move, which was followed not much later by my passing into the twelfth grade, I picked up an acute inner
ear infection while on an extended weekend outing
(by bike and with a girl) into the Bergische Land on a
sleety Shrove Tuesday. This infection kept me in bed
far beyond Easter. When I was allowed to get up
again, my love had evaporated (yes, a pity, but it had
simply evaporated), and I was moved up to the twelfth,
with the serious warning that I would have to work
hard.

I did, I caught up with the class, became used to
my new, quiet route to school: Karolinger-Ring,
Sachsen-Ring, Ulrich-Gasse, Vor den Siebenbürgen,
Schnur-Gasse (past the pawnshop), a few yards along
Martinsfeld as far as Heinrich-Strasse, which I now
entered from the other, very quiet end. The worry
about "what's to become of the boy?" grew ever more
serious, more justified. Heinen, before disappearing
out of the country, had also participated in the discus-

sion and suggested the career of librarian, but he had
forgotten about the book-burnings, and wasn't the profession of librarian an endangered one? Was I sup-
posed to spend my life lending out Hanns Johst or
Hans Friedrich Blunck, or concerning myself with the
collected articles of Heinz Steguweit? After I had rejected a libarian's career, someone in my family—I
don't know who—came up with the idea that it should
be "something to do with books." Too bad that, given
the circumstances, the boy couldn't be persuaded to
take an interest in theology.

14

THAT SUMMER, shortly after the move, which en-
tailed the usual chaos (new curtains for the big
windows, allocation of rooms, frequent, and fruitless
family budget councils), I went off on my bike, by
myself on a sort of study trip via Mainz, Würzburg,
through the Spessart and Steigerwald hills to Bamberg;
and, since I wished to avoid the mixture of Hitler Youth
and League of German Girls in the youth hostels, my
father obtained a letter of introduction for me to the
"Kolping houses" along the way. As an old member of
the Kolping (a Catholic guild of journeymen-artisans),
he had good connections with its headquarters in

Cologne. This meant I had access to cheap bed-and-
breakfast; I also became acquainted with the activities
of the Kolping Brothers, and gratefully accepted coffee and bread, soup and milk, in canteens from the
hands of South German nuns.

Mainz: that broad-hipped Romanesque cathedral
of red sandstone was more to my liking than Cologne
Cathedral; even in Cologne I had felt greater affinity
with the gray Romanesque churches. My father was a
good guide through churches and museums. And for
me, coming as I did from an almost completely un-
Baroque city, Würzburg was both alien and pleasing:
a different world, "occupied" not only by churches
and palaces but also by Leonhard Frank's *Robber
Band*, which we boys had devoured. In Bamberg I was
surprised by the coolness of the statue of my namesake
to which I was really making a pilgrimage. The
princely horseman, whose picture probably hung over
the desk or bed of almost every young German, seemed
cold to me, clever and competent—he inspired no
affection in me. When I got home, I took down his
picture from the wall and put it in a drawer. Devout
Catholic though he was, he seemed to me—I couldn't
help it—"somehow Protestant," and, after all, *Catholic* was what we wanted to be and to remain, in spite
of all our derisive laughter and abuse. That was why
the appearance, shortly before the end of 1936, of
Léon Bloy's *Blood of the Poor* hit us like a bombshell,

a long way indeed from the Dostoievski bombshell, yet in its effect, similar to it. Add to this the pyrotechnics of Chesterton—a strange mixture, I know, into which German literature, even the banned and officially disgraced literature, didn't enter. *Buddenbrooks* did, peripherally, but someone like Tucholsky not at all; Kästner yes. For the rest, though, everything smacked of "Berlin," and Berlin was not loved, was even less loved since the Nazis had taken it over. Unfair, I know (meanwhile I have learned a bit more).

15

FOR SOME TIME now an innovation for secondary schools had existed: training camps. The oldest students from two different schools would spend three weeks together in a youth hostel so as to become acquainted with each other, the countryside, and the local people, as well as attending lectures and taking part in marches and sports. I participated fully in the first one, in Zülpich, where we joined the parallel class of Aloysius College. Father Hubert Becher, that kindly, cultured Jesuit, had a mitigating influence. We marched through the vast sugarbeet fields of that "Merovingian land," visited Roman ruins, felt the spirit of Chlodwig. We went over an old textile factory

in Euskirchen where bales and bales of army cloth
were being produced. I passed up another camp in
Oberwesel—I forget whether it was the last or the last
but one—by more or less extorting an impressive med-
ical certificate from our family doctor. Then there was
another one in Ludweiler near Völklingen on the Saar
at which I stayed for half the time, but there the loud-
mouthed Hitler Youth mentality was already so prevalent that I lost my nerve and simply went home. In
Ludweiler the writer Johannes Kirchweng read to us
from his works. He didn't seem—to me at any rate—
entirely at ease with the whole thing, and by "thing"
I mean all that Nazi business and those claims to lost
German territory. Johannes Kirchweng, worker's son
and Catholic priest, seemed a nice fellow, but tired and
sad, probably didn't quite trust his recent fame and
was already foreseeing its abuse. He read from an
autobiographical novel in which he described the harsh
conditions of his father's working world, that of a
glassblower. He did not, as I have just discovered,
reach a great age: at his death in 1951 he was fifty-
one, so in 1935 or 1936 he must have been thirty-five
or thirty-six. I remember him as a very old man, a nice
fellow and tired (and that reminds me of Heinrich
Lersch, whose novel *Hammer Blows* was also about his
father and *his* craft, that of a boilermaker).

In the taverns of Ludweiler or Völklingen, work-
men would tell us in whispers that, instead of being

able to buy French Riz-La cigarette paper for five pfennigs, they now had to pay fifteen pfennigs for the German Gizeh paper; but of course, they said, they weren't Frenchmen, you know, they were Germans of course, you know. Völklingen, the Röchling steel works, the strikes and all that, and why didn't we take a look at the foundry? It certainly wasn't pleasant or edifying: it smelled of poverty, stale, of a stifling all-pervading Catholicism. There was also—and not only because of the cigarette paper—a certain wistfulness expressed not openly but in whispers.

And in the evening at the youth hostel there was all that whooping and hollering of the triumphant Hitler Youth, and their threats against us—me and my friend Caspar Markard—because when they sang the Horst Wessel Song we would start up with: "If all are now unfaithful, then faithful we'll remain." I lost my nerve (as often happened later), I suppose one might say I was "hypersensitive"—or was I more than just an outsider, was I already an eccentric? At any rate, I simply went home, again with a taste of things to come. Yes, we sang: "If all are now unfaithful," and I wrote not only love poems but patriotic ones too, and I read Stefan George, whom I never for a moment regarded as a Nazi. Caspar Markard had been expelled from Brühl High School on account of political remarks and activities that were dubbed "Communist," and our school had accepted him.

16

It MUST NOT be forgotten that we were moving toward war. I bought Barbusse and Remarque. Barbusse impressed me more than Remarque. In school—that's how it seemed, or how it seems to me today—the last vestiges of strictness, of severity even, disappeared, the kind that had been prevalent from teacher to student. There were arguments, but they were between younger and older *adults;* they were serious ones, they had lost their schoolboy character.

Our math teacher, Mr. Müllenmeister (known as MM), who was considered unusually strict and bore the marks of World War I but never talked about it, proved to be the mildest of all: during the late summer and fall he hardly disguised his efforts to familiarize us with the geometry and algebra questions we might expect in our final exams. In the eleventh grade, almost a third of the class, five or six students, had been failed, perhaps because the school wished to present a trim, secure graduating class: thirteen of us remained, awaiting graduation. That last school summer, the last school fall, seem to have lasted forever. There was not only the cultural pilgrimage to the statue of Heinrich II in Bamberg, not only the usual preparations for our final exams during which, using dictionaries as a concordance, we tried to work out what Latin and Greek texts to expect: there were also the Olympic Games, with the enormous, utterly depressing propaganda success, both at home and abroad, of the Nazis. And in a "postlude" in the Cologne stadium we saw the totally un-Germanic Olympic winners Jesse Owens and Ralph Metcalfe, the latter making the sign of the cross before the start of the race. A champion who was a Catholic and a Negro!

That summer my friend Caspar Markard took me along to meet Robert Grosche, the priest who had retired from the city to live in the country at Vochem near Brühl, where he used to receive a small group of students for a sort of weekly seminar. Grosche, the classic Rhinelander, the classic, highly educated abbé, the Claudel translator and expert, one of Germany's first truly ecumenical priests, yet intensely Roman: his study, crammed with books and always filled with pipe smoke, was an island that fascinated and at the same time intimidated me. We discussed "salvation arising from the Jews," he lent us books to which he had drawn our attention. As a sideline Grosche was also editor of the Cologne bookdealers' "literary guide." Those were unforgettable evenings. Grosche was very West European yet very German, with a surprising admixture of nationalism; very Catholic, witty, of high caliber, courageous. We were sure he was a "born" cardinal, born to be the future Bishop of Cologne. But no: when Cardinal Schulte died, he was followed by Frings. Maybe Grosche was too lofty for the Vatican, perhaps even too cultured, and whether he would have suited the Nazis, who, according to the Concordat, had a say in the matter, is uncertain.

Here I will permit myself a brief speculation beyond the year 1937: Grosche, rather than Frings, Cardinal and Archbishop of Cologne after 1945; Grosche, who certainly favored and would have favored the Christian Democrats, as the decisive figure beside Adenauer in German postwar Catholicism? Things would have turned out differently. Whether better is something I dare not say. Even in those days, on leaving that marvelous, comfortable Vochem study, full of books and tobacco smoke, to go home to Cologne by train or on my bike, I would feel a bit intimidated by so much cultured composure, by that hint of nationalism, and the unmistakable if gentle overripeness of the bourgeoisie. It was tremendous to be there, to be with him, but it was not what I was looking for.

Our own family were turning their backs more and more on the bourgeoisie, and Grosche's study, equipped in the classic manner with piles of books and journals, and all that saturated culture flowing toward us from the lectures given by the Catholic Academic League—all that was not only well meant but also helpful, and it was good; yet I knew, or rather, merely suspected, that I didn't belong there.

At home, things were far from always being "comfortable": that explosive mixture of petty-bourgeois vestiges, Bohemian traits, and proletarian pride, not truly belonging to any class, yet arrogant rather than humble, in other words almost "class conscious" again. And of course, of course, in spite of everything, Catholic, Catholic, Catholic. There was no room for that "confounded" serenity of existence *sub specie æternitatis*. We lived *sub specie ætatis*. And I don't know whether I am in trouble again with my synchronization in assuming that it was during that summer that we became addicted to Pervitin, unwittingly—at least my mother, my older sister, and I did; the rest of the family didn't. The brother of a friend, a doctor, told us about this "stuff" used in hospitals, where they put it into the coffee of obstinate malingerers to encourage them to leave voluntarily. Apparently the "stuff" worked, and we bought it. Today it is one of the most strictly controlled prescription stimulants, but in those days it could be bought over the counter in any pharmacy: thirty tablets for 1.86 marks. We took it, and it worked: it induced a tremendous euphoria, and we could use some euphoria; it had a drier, I might almost say "more spiritual," effect than alcohol. (I used it well into the war, obtaining prescriptions for it from a young woman with whom I was friendly, a doctor's assistant, after prescriptions became required. Thank God I ran out of supplies one day, and I kicked the habit. It was dangerous stuff, and one of our best friends succumbed to it.)

Again and again our electricity was cut off, a harsh penalty for a family of such voracious readers: candles were expensive and quickly burned down, and my mother received such dire warnings on account of her tamperings with meter seals that in the end she desisted. It was just at that time that I began to feel so alien to the cozy atmosphere at Grosche's, legitimate and gracious though it was.

17

WHATEVER HAPPENED, I didn't want to jeopardize my graduation, didn't want to risk too much. For economic reasons, among others, that would have been irresponsible, and, besides, I was simply fed up with school. It was time to put an end to it and enter the deluge that was facing us. Then, right into the midst of my preparations for my final exams, a minor bombshell was dropped: that year the Nazis reduced the secondary school period by one year to eight years; but we had already done nine years, which meant we practically had our graduation in our pockets. The

worst that could have happened—failing our final
exams—would have meant taking them again two or
three months later with the class immediately below
us. In that case, failure was unlikely, since it would
have meant that the school had declared someone to be
ready for the twelfth grade who would drop back to
the tenth-grade level. Since the dreaded written tests
had been eliminated, it was merely a matter of finding
volunteers for the oral tests in the tough subjects of
Latin, Greek, and math, so that no one who was weak
in those areas would risk being tested in one of them.
We came quite openly to an arrangement with our
teachers, and at the advice, at the urging almost, of
Mr. Bauer I took on Latin; in return he as good as
promised not to test me on Juvenal, whom we were then
studying.

I don't know whether Juvenal was in our curriculum, or whether Bauer had recognized how topical
he was and had chosen him for that reason: in Juvenal,
arbitrariness, despotism, depravity, corruption of political mores, the decline of the Republican idea, were
described with ample clarity, including even a few
"June 30's," staged by the Praetorians, and allusions
to Tigellinus. Then, without looking for it, I came
across in a secondhand book bin a Juvenal translation
with a detailed commentary, published in 1838. The
commentary was almost twice as long as the text and
made thrilling historical reading, besides being amus-

ing for its Romantic vocabulary. I couldn't afford that
copious tome but bought it anyhow, and it is one of the
few books I managed to bring safely through the war
and did *not* sacrifice to the black market afterward.
(In those days—a forbidden look forward to 1945—
there was a class of profiteers who had everything except books, which they urgently needed to decorate
their fine walls, and we unloaded everything that we
knew would be republished: an autographed copy of
Buddenbrooks, for example, brought me a tidy little
sum!)

I hung onto my Juvenal. In the twelfth grade I
didn't use it as an aid to translation, that would have
been against my principles: I merely devoured the
commentary, which read like a thriller. In Greek we
read *Antigone.* That needed no commentary, not even
a knowing wink; and, as I have said, the tiring monot-
ony of translating in class (Oh, the bent, bored backs
of those who were forced to go through a classical high
school! Why, I wonder?) made me impatient, and I
would sit down at home with the dictionary and read
on ahead. Brief appearances in class of Gerhard Nebel
as a substitute teacher brought a little fire and a re-
freshing gust of anarchy; for the first time I heard
about the Jünger brothers. It was said—and probably
correctly—that Nebel had been transferred for dis-
ciplinary reasons. He also taught gym and boxing, in
neither of which I took part. He claimed, fairly openly,

that the recent introduction of boxing was due to a
secret, repressed anglophilia on the part of the Nazis.
Within a few years the Nazis closed down the school
for good—which speaks for the school.

We ostentatiously took part in the penitent pil-
grimages of the men of Cologne that led from the
Heumarkt to the Kalk Chapel and back—tolerated by
the Nazis and watched by informers.

Here I must mention, as a little epitaph for one of
Cologne's first air-raid victims, our friend Hans S.,
who owned a beaver collar. This collar was our last,
our very last reserve when we couldn't scrape up any
more money and had nothing more to pawn; it brought
in two marks at the pawnshop, and that meant three
movie tickets and two packs of cigarettes, or four
movie tickets without cigarettes, or four concert tickets
—and we went to the movies a lot: it was dark in there,
and even the Nazis had to keep quiet and were not
distinguishable.

18

OUR SCHOOLDAYS seemed to be drawing to a peaceful close; the arrangements with our teachers had been
made. In the choice of careers, which had to be declared for inclusion in our graduation certificates, it

turned out that we were the first graduating class in
living memory, if not since the school's existence, not
to provide a theologian. Traditionally the school had
been a reliable supplier for the theological seminaries
in Bonn. The fact that we sent no one there could have
had nothing to do with the Nazis, for the class following us was once again a supplier. And it happened to
be in religion that our schooldays came to a nasty
rather than a peaceful close.

Among the members of the Hitler Youth, the Storm
Troopers, and the S.S., there were, of course, not only
superficial opportunists but also true believers, believers both as as Nazis and as Catholics, and there
were conflicts that we discussed in class, such as obedi-
ence, the Day of the German Mother (which our teacher
of religion buried in a theologically convincing
manner), and, since he was neither stupid nor humor-
less nor in the slightest degree opportunistic, something in the nature of a "skeptical trust" had been
formed: we knew where we stood with each other, and
there were neither boorish gibes nor denunciations.
But all this was destroyed in a single hour, when he
felt himself obliged or—as I am more inclined to
believe since he did it with such painful reluctance—
was obliged by the curriculum to enlighten us on sex-
ual matters. Maybe that "enlightenment" had been on
the twelfth-grade curriculum since 1880; I can't
imagine the Cologne high school graduates of 1880

being any less enlightened than we were. Be that as it
may, he did it, he enlightened us: blushing with em-
barrassment, keeping his eyelids lowered, he spoke
about the fact of there being two different sexes. He
spoke with dignity, not ludicrously at all, and we were
still disposed to concede that he was carrying out this
long overdue task with a painful sense of duty.

But then came the moment of disaster when, in
connection with the sex organs and their functions, he
spoke of "strawberries and whipped cream." The
youngest among us was at least eighteen, the oldest
twenty-two, and we had grown up in a city famous and
notorious not only for its sanctity but also for its tradi-
tion of widespread and widely varied prostitution.
Whereas during the less embarrassing parts of his talk,
during the awkward, stammered explanations, we had
just managed to suppress our laughter, now it burst
forth: cynical, cruel, almost lethal. Even the most
hardened among us—and there were some hardened
ones, of course—felt this comparison to be both an
insult and a slur on their experiences, no matter how
"dirty" these may have been. Our revenge was ap-
palling: five filthy jokes were each reduced to a key
word plus a number; word and number were written
on the blackboard; and in the few remaining religion
classes someone would mention one of the five numbers, whereupon the whole class remembered the entire obscenity and burst out laughing. I admit to having

shared not only in the laughter but also in the choice
and condensing of the obscenities.

During this cruel game, our teacher—and in retro-
spect I have to admire him—never lost his sense of
humor, wanted to share in the cause of our laughter,
went to the blackboard and read out—Oh disaster!—
key words and numbers, looked at us in puzzlement,
asked why we were laughing. It was cruel: a totally
innocent man was being crucified, but perhaps that
kind of innocent person should not be charged with
enlightening twelfth-graders. It should not have been
permitted: that "strawberries and whipped cream"
was an insult to anyone who had or knew a girl;
culinary comparisons in this "area" cannot be anything but revolting. As a further revenge, some of us
brought binoculars to class to observe the somewhat
inadequately dressed ladies in the rear windows of the
buildings along Perlen-Graben, as they leaned out
their kitchen windows or hung washing on their laun-
dry racks, facing the school yard—permanent objects
of young male curiosity, and we would comment on
their visible feminine charms and their petticoats. In
those days bras were not yet so common.

If I have since found that *almost nothing* of our
music and drawing lessons has remained with me, I
have no wish to blame the teachers for this: it is sad
and a pity, and I am still suffering from that "wasted
time." Perhaps it was because the "social status" of

those teachers as non-academics among academics—
that deplorable German resentment—made them and
us uncertain. I can't help it: *almost nothing* has
remained.

In December I started sending off applications for
an apprenticeship in a bookstore: handwritten, with a
photo, of course, and a notarized copy of my pre-
graduation report, which my sister Gertrud obtained
for me. All that cost money and, moreover, destroyed
one illusion: obviously I would at the very least be
automatically absorbed into the Nazi Labor Front. I
dreamed of some quiet bookstore, not too big, with an
owner who at least wasn't a Nazi. It was not so easy to
find an apprenticeship: there was no economic miracle
in that particular field. But finally I did find a shop,
quiet, not too big, and not even remotely Nazi: on the
contrary, neither the boss nor any of the staff was of
that stripe, and I made a good friend there!

When it came, the final exam was not much more
than a formality; it started at eight in the morning,
and by one or two o'clock everything was over, for all
of us. We were taken in alphabetical order, so my turn
came first; I was given a passage from Cicero, was told
all the words I didn't know, and passed. Regulations
required that I also be examined in biology (everyone
was examined in biology), so I reeled off the Mendelian laws, drew the appropriate red, white, and pink
circles on the blackboard. I was through by eight

thirty. At lunchtime we met for a glass of beer in a tavern: it was all over. I didn't even bother to attend the graduation ceremony: my brother Alfred, who went there for a class reunion, accepted the certificate on my behalf and brought it home.

Sometimes I still wonder whether the manufacturers of school supplies noticed a boom in pink chalk: in how many thousands of schools—and not only during final exams—was Mendelian pink drawn on the blackboard by how many hundreds of thousands of students?

A NOTE ABOUT THE AUTHOR

Heinrich Böll is the first German to win the Nobel Prize for literature since Thomas Mann in 1929. Born in Cologne, Germany, in 1917, Böll was reared in a liberal Catholic, pacifist family. Drafted into the Wehrmacht, he served on the Russian and French fronts and was wounded four times before he found himself in an American prisoner-of-war camp. After the war, he enrolled in the University of Cologne, but dropped out to write about his shattering experiences as a soldier. His first novel, *The Train Was on Time*, was published in 1949, and he went on to become one of the most prolific and important of the postwar German writers. His best-known novels include *Billiards at Half-Past Nine*, *The Clown*, *Group Portrait with Lady*, and, most recently, *The Safety Net*. He is also famous as a writer of short stories. Böll is past president of International P.E.N. and is a leading defender of the intellectual freedom of writers throughout the world. He and his wife divide their time between Cologne and a farmhouse in the Eifel mountains.

A NOTE ON THE TYPE

This book is composed in Bodoni, a typeface named after Giambattista Bodoni (1740–1813), a printer of Parma and an innovator in type design. The face is a modern version, based on a composite conception of the Bodoni manner rather than on any particular one of Bodoni's many fonts.

Composed by Maryland Linotype Composition Company,
Baltimore, Maryland.
Printed and bound by
The Maple-Vail Book Manufacturing Group,
York, Pennsylvania.